Sutton Free Pub...
P.O. Box ...
4 Uxbridge R...
Sutton, MA 01590

GRILL MY CHEESE

NISHA PATEL & NISHMA CHAUHAN

GRILL MY CHEESE

THE COOKBOOK

FROM SLUMDOG GRILLIONAIRE TO JUSTIN BRIEBER: THE GREATEST TOASTED CHEESE SANDWICHES EVER!

quadrille

A TRUE FRIEND IS SOMEONE WHO THINKS YOU'RE A GOOD CHEESE EVEN IF YOU'RE HALF BLUE

We are two friends who love cheese. There is NOTHING better than melted cheese oozing out of golden buttery bread.

Food has always been a huge part of our lives, but it wasn't until we moved in together that we really developed a passion for creating delicious cheese toasties. In May 2013, we decided to follow our hearts (and our stomachs) and open Grill My Cheese.

Our friends and family got the goods of our experiments and after some great feedback from them, we decided to hit the streets. We began our journey at a council-run market in West London. After a horrific first day trading (tears, tantrums and failing equipment) we discovered people were excited by our menu and genuinely wanted to eat our food. We were thrilled! Street food was the ideal platform for us to get started on our journey and although it hasn't been plain sailing, we wouldn't change it. So this is us, still learning, still eating and having an amazing time as we go along (as cheesy as that may sound).

This book is all about trying new ideas. Although there is always a place for a standard white bread toastie, we knew we could do better. Taking inspiration from classic combinations and the foods we love, we make them our own, creating sandwiches like the Slumdog Grillionaire. This is based on both our mums' recipes with our own special twist – our take on a Bombay sandwich.

We also love sweet and salty combinations. One of our favourites is the PB&J but don't forget to give the Doughnut Grilled Cheese a go, too.

We set out to make people happy with our food. There's no better feeling than when someone comes up to us and says it was the best toastie they've ever had. We are so excited to be able to share our recipes with you in this book and hope you feel the same when you try them at home.

Nisha Patel & Nishma Chauhan

OUR TEN COMMANDMENTS OF GRILLED CHEESE

1 DO IT YOUR WHEY

There is no such thing as the 'perfect' toastie. Everyone has their own version, and we hope these recipes will give you the inspiration to create your ideal toastie.

2 MORE IS MORE

Spending a little more on your ingredients will make a big difference to your grilled cheese. There is always a time and place for the nostalgic 'white bread' toastie. It's a comforting classic. That being said, you deserve better.

3 BUTTER ME UP

Buttering the outside of your bread is a MUST to ensure a golden buttery crust. We recommend using a small amount of unsalted butter.

4 CHEESE ME BABY

Melty, Stretchy, Cheesy – this is what you want from your grilled cheese. Experiment with different cheeses.

GRATE EXPECTATIONS

Without getting too scientific (not really), cheese melts quicker when it's grated. Ultimately, resulting in a perfect cook, especially when you add more ingredients.

MIX IT UP

Hams, jams and pickles – most things taste better with cheese. Play around with different flavour combinations and don't be afraid to try new things. Some of our best sandwiches have come from having fun with flavours.

CHEASON' IT

All our sauces and chutneys work great with grilled cheese, either inside or as dips.

GRILLING ME SOFTLY

Cook on a medium heat to ensure your sandwich is golden on the outside and fully melted to gooey perfection.

HALLOU-IT'S NOT-MI

There are very few don'ts to making a grilled cheese. The main one is using hard cheeses that don't melt, such as halloumi and paneer. Cottage cheese is also a no no. We do use some 'non-melty' cheeses in some of our sandwiches, such as ricotta and cream cheese. These add texture and richness.

BRIE-LIEVE IT

Grilled cheese is simple and honest. Don't take it too seriously, it should always be made with love.

THE BREAD

When it comes down to it, the humble cheese toastie is made using three vital ingredients, bread being one of them. There needs to be enough texture to withstand the mounds of melted cheese and all the crispy bits.

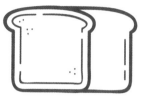

SOURDOUGH

Our personal favourite. We find sourdough the best type of bread for a grilled cheese sandwich – its slightly sour flavour cuts through some of the richness of the cheese, and its firm and slightly waxy consistency makes it sturdy enough to hold all your components together. The fantastic air pockets also mean loads of cheesy crispy bits post grilling. There are many sourdoughs you can use and even mixed flour sourdoughs (which are more likely to come in a friendlier shaped loaf). We recommend you buy your loaves sliced, and would suggest a medium thickness of about 12mm (½ inch) as an optimum.

FARMHOUSE

Sometimes, there is nothing better than white bread for a cheese toastie. Growing up on generic supermarket white sliced is something we all remember and it does bring you back to the nostalgic toasties of your younger years. Fortunately, we now live in a time where great bread is more accessible. If you must (and sometimes you really must) use white bread, then a farmhouse loaf is that little bit more special than a generic supermarket brand. The soft doughy yieldyness of the bread really soaks up all the cheese and gives you a great crisp and crunchy toastie. We recommend a thick slice for these recipes. Granary and wholemeal also work well.

BLOOMER

Most supermarket bloomers will be very similar to farmhouse loaves, the only difference being that they are free-formed, meaning they are allowed to prove without a tin. However, if you get a good bakery bloomer, then you will get something slightly different – a denser loaf with a thicker crust. This makes it a great bread for toasties and sandwiches, as, like with sourdough, there is enough sturdiness to hold the components. The bloomer is also given a longer proving time, sometimes overnight, and, – as with sourdough – this results in a much more flavourful bread and a beautiful, pillowy white interior. A bloomer works well with all the recipes in this book, unless otherwise stated.

CIABATTA

More traditionally used in cafés up and down the country, the ciabatta works as a good foundation for most of these toastie recipes. There are many variations of ciabatta throughout Italy, some with a dense crumb and some with more air pockets. The ciabatta that is most commonly used outside Italy, however, is a spongy soft bread, slightly chewy, which crisps up once toasted.

RYE

A full-flavoured loaf. Go for a dark rye for all of its malty flavour. Rye bread is usually a lot denser than normal wheat bread loaves and works well in simple toasties – any from the Easy Cheesy section (see page 20) would work well with rye. Traditional rye bread is made very much like sourdough, using a starter and slow fermentation. Any rye breads using a mixture of both rye and wheat flour will be much lighter and more like wheat bread in texture.

BRIOCHE

We love brioche, mostly because it's packed with loads of butter. When it comes to our recipes, however, we would only suggest having it with simple fillings (mostly in the Easy Cheesy section, page 20) or toasted with our ice cream on top or inside it. There is a high fat content in brioche, so, depending on the grilling method, the toastie could be very greasy and very flat. We suggest toasting lightly in a frying pan and using slightly less cheese than we have suggested in these recipes. Available as buns and a loaf, it also works well with burgers, fried eggs and our candy bacon butter (see page 133).

FRUIT LOAF

For our sweet toasties, a fruit loaf works best. Most fruit loaves are smaller than regular loaves, making them the perfect size for a dessert. Our sweet treats are quite rich, and having them made up in a smaller portion is ideal. The loaf is not overly sweet, and is sturdy enough to toast, providing a great base. Cinnamon loaves also work well in this instance.

GLUTEN-FREE BREAD

As of yet, we have sadly not been able to find a great gluten-free substitute for our toasties on the stall. The breads we have sampled have either been too cake-like, with the crumb too delicate, or too sweet. But, of course, if you do have any intolerances then use whatever substitute you like best.

THE CHEESE

Now for the second most important ingredient, the cheese. In order to figure out the best combination of cheese for your toastie at home, we have broken it down into three simple categories. There will be some overlap in some of the categories, as a number of 'cheesers' are good 'melters', but if you ensure you have a good ratio of each in your blend, you are bound to have a winning toastie.

1) Cheesers: These are cheeses with a stronger flavour profile and are there predominantly to give flavour to your toastie.

2) Melters: A toastie is not a toastie without melted cheese. Some cheese, no matter how much you try, will not fully melt. This includes the likes of halloumi and paneer.

3) Stretchers: These are a must for getting melted cheese on your chin. Everyone loves to 'pull' a grilled cheese and see the web of cheese strings.

CHEESERS

Blue Cheese The softer ones (like dolcelatte or Castello Blue) are rich, creamy and almost sweet like caramel, with the harder varieties sharp and salty. Great on a cheese board or in a salad, blue cheese is incredibly versatile. It can be spread, crumbled or melted into sauces.

Chèvre Goat's Cheese A generic French term for goat's cheese, chèvre comes in many forms, with the most common being a slightly crumbly and creamy fresh cheese with a complex, buttery flavour profile.

Comté A French pale yellow, creamy cheese often likened to Gruyère, this is matured in the darkness of caves and aged for a minimum of four months and up to 24 months. Considered to be one of the finest cheeses in the world, it has a great melt with notes of roasted nuts, fruity pepper and brown butter, with a sweet finish.

Cream Cheese Soft, mild-tasting cheese made from milk and cream, this is incredibly versatile and can be used in sweet and savoury foods. A slick of cream cheese in a grilled cheese adds an indulgence factor that, once you try it, will change your life.

Feta This Greek soft-brined cheese is creamy and crumbly with a sharp, salty and almost sour finish. It is very good in salads, but when melted becomes creamier. It works really well paired with sweet olives.

Gouda A Dutch semi-hard cheese that is renowned for its rich, unique flavour. It has a mild, salty yet fruity flavour with a sweet finish and elastic texture.

Manchego A rich, creamy, firm Spanish sheep's cheese with a mildly gamey flavour and a hazelnutty sweetness. The flavour varies significantly depending on age – the younger the cheese, the more supple and moist in texture with a fruity, tangy note. As it matures, there is a more caramel, nutty and almost sweet taste. It is aged for up to a year and becomes more crumbly.

Parmesan A hard, granular Italian cheese with a rich umami flavour that is also fruity and nutty.

Ricotta This Italian soft fresh cheese can be used in both sweet and savoury dishes. It is low in fat but carries a creamy texture that is mild in flavour.

MELTERS

American Cheese Also known as 'processed cheese', made from a blend of milk, solids, fat and whey concentrates. This is your typical Kraft/Dairylea slices but it also comes in tube form (Velveeta/Cheez Whiz). It has a mild, salty and faintly sweet flavour and a low melting point. The taste and texture vary by brand.

Brie Named the 'Queen of Cheese', this French soft cheese is pale in colour with a white edible rind. Buttery, runny and soft-ripened with a mild, slightly fruity and nutty taste, it is a great, versatile cheese. There are many varieties of Brie, now made internationally, but only Brie de Meaux and Brie de Melun can be classified as Brie. There is a great British version called Waterloo.

Cheddar There are many types of Cheddar, ranging from mild to medium and extra mature, but as a general rule, they are all great melters. They can be an excellent way of adding flavour to your toastie; this will depend on the type you choose. Mild Cheddars are gentle and creamy in flavour, with mature versions tending to be sweet and nutty, with a longer finish. You can even get smoked Cheddars as well as Cheddars that have been blended with herbs or flavourings.

Double Gloucester A traditional semi-hard cheese with a smooth, buttery texture and a rich, nutty flavour. Typically aged for four months, you will find that the more aged the cheese, the more complex the flavour and harder it becomes.

Aged Goat's Cheese We are referring here to the soft variety covered in an edible ash. It has a fluffy middle with a gooey texture when left at room temperature. Creamy with a strong flavour profile, it works well with caramelized onions and roasted vegetables.

Gruyère A hard, yellow, semi-smelly Swiss cheese, Gruyère is buttery sweet with a slightly salty finish and, as with most cheeses, its flavour becomes more robust with age.

Provolone An Italian semi-soft smoked cheese that intensifies when melted. Typically used in a lot of Italo-American cooking, it is rich, milky and mildly nutty, with a sharp saltiness.

Raclette A French cheese commonly served melted over potatoes and pickles.

Reblochon Known to be a devotional cheese offered to Carthusian monks by farmers in the 1500s in return for the monks blessing their crops, this great tasting melter is used in the dish tartiflette (which is DELICIOUS).

Red Leicester Formally known as Leicestershire cheese, this hard, pressed cheese with a rich orange colour has a sweet, mellow flavour with a creamy texture. A great alternative to Cheddar, it melts well and, like most cheeses, gets stronger in flavour the longer it matures.

STRETCHERS

Buffalo Mozzarella The kind you will find in bags or tubs of water to retain its freshness. Made with the milk of a water buffalo, it is a soft, delicate cheese with a unique stretchiness when melted. One of our favourite cheeses, with its milky, creamy flavour profile, it works really well un-melted in salads or alone with a drizzle of good olive oil and some black pepper.

Mozzarella (low moisture) This is the kind you find in supermarkets, in blocks or pre-grated packs. It is much firmer than fresh mozzarella, due to the curds being left to sour slightly before being placed in hot water to loosen the protein structure and then left to dry out. Slightly salty and dense, it carries very little flavour unless melted, but has a great stretch that makes it perfect for melting.

Emmental Yellow, mild, fruity-flavoured hard Swiss cheese known for its holey characteristics. When melted it has a buttery taste often likened to Gruyère, and is commonly used in fondue.

Fontina Semi-soft Italian cheese with a pungent smell, quite unlike its balanced, complex flavour. Rich and creamy with a slight fruity taste, it has an elastic texture that produces the perfect stretch when melted. Considered to be Italy's answer to Gruyère, you will also find varieties made by the US and Denmark. American fontina is more yellow in colour and less aged, resulting in a buttery taste.

Taleggio Semi-soft, stinky Italian cheese with a sticky rind that is great when crisped up on top of a macaroni cheese. Despite the smell, the flavour is balanced, complex and nutty, with a slight saltiness. Once left at room temperature or melted, it becomes oozy and glorious.

OUR BLEND

At Grill My Cheese, we use a signature blend of four different cheeses that we have created to give the best flavour, melt and stretch. It is a blend that works great on its own but at the same time has been created to complement all the other fillings we use.

Keen's Cheddar (1 part) – an unpasteurized, strong-flavoured Cheddar matured for a minimum of one year. It has a creamy, smooth and firm texture and long, earthy, rich, nutty flavours with a sharp finish.

Farmhouse mature Cheddar (2 parts) – a great flavour enhancer to mellow out the blend slightly.

Swiss Gruyère (1 part) – a buttery, sweet, slightly nutty cheese with a flavour that varies widely with age. We use one of the younger varieties; the more mature it is, the more earthy and complex the flavour.

Cow's 'low moisture' mozzarella (2 parts) – known for its mild flavour and great 'stretch', this is one of the most versatile and best cheeses to use when adding stronger flavours to a toastie (see opposite).

COOKING METHODS

The goal when making any toastie is to make sure you have an even, golden, buttery crust and a gooey pile of melted cheese in the centre. When adding other fillings, they also need to be heated through. If you get the heat wrong, you could be left with a burnt, unmelted or soggy toastie.

BUTTERING THE BREAD

We use a tiny amount of butter on the outside of our toasties. Our cheese blend has a decent fat content so we don't want our toasties to be greasy and cloying. By using a scant buttering, we assure you that you will get a golden buttery crust without any of the excess grease. Unsalted butter is our recommended choice.

WHAT WE USE: GRILL AND MEAT PRESS

To cook the sandwiches on the stall we use a flat-top grill (plancha), with some traditional meat presses. These can be purchased online (we had ours shipped in from the US) and they cook bacon, steak and other meat really well. These presses can also be used instead of the spatula in the frying pan method below.

OUR FAVOURITE AT-HOME METHOD: FRYING PAN AND WEIGHT

When making a single toastie, or a few for friends, we would recommend the frying pan method. Everyone has a frying pan (we hope), and all you require is a spatula and some patience.

Heat your frying pan to a medium heat and place your toastie in the dry pan. Either push down gently with a spatula, or use a saucepan (or any other weight) to hold the toastie down. This ensures an even cook with melted cheese in the middle. Depending on the fillings, the toastie should take about 3 minutes a side.

PANINI PRESS / GEORGE FOREMAN

Place the prepared sandwich in the grill and cook on a medium heat for 3–4 minutes, depending on the strength of your machine. The good thing about panini presses is that they are generally easy to check for 'toastie readiness'. We prefer flat plates (they're easier to clean), but ridged plates also work just as well, and give you a slightly crunchier toastie. All breads work well in the panini machine.

TOASTIE MACHINE

There are only certain types of bread that work in this machine, and a white or brown standard sliced loaf would be our only suggestion. The machine can either deliver nostalgic wonders, or result in molten cheese explosions and soggy crusts.

Always use pre-softened butter on the outside of the bread to avoid any rips in the bread. Don't overfill your sandwiches if you're using this cooking method, as the machine does restrict how much filling you can fit inside your toastie. Make up your toastie as per the recipe and then carefully place inside your toastie machine. Close the clip and leave to toast for 4–5 minutes. The sandwich is ready when the bread has crisped up into two beautiful triangle pockets. Leave to cool for a while before taking your first bite; the steam inside the toastie could lead to serious injury.

Given the nature of this method, the sandwiches that won't work as well are the Fresh Tuna Melt (see page 42) and any of the dessert grilled cheeses.

OVEN

You'll need two heavy-duty baking trays. Heat the first tray (the bottom) in an oven preheated to 180°C/350°F/Gas 4, upside down as it's the bottom of the tray that will be used to put the sandwiches on. All the sandwiches need to be ready and prepped on the side as, once the preheated tray comes out, they need to be placed on it quickly. Depending on the size of your tray, you could get a number of toasties out at the same time this way. Place the sandwiches on the bottom tray, stick another tray on top, the right way up, so that the toasties are weighed down, and bake in the oven for 10–15 minutes, depending on your fillings. You should have evenly cooked sandwiches, all ready at the same time to feed your awaiting guests.

TOASTER BAGS

Simple and easy. Place your desired toastie in the toaster bag and follow the bag instructions. We recommend using for classic cheese toasties.

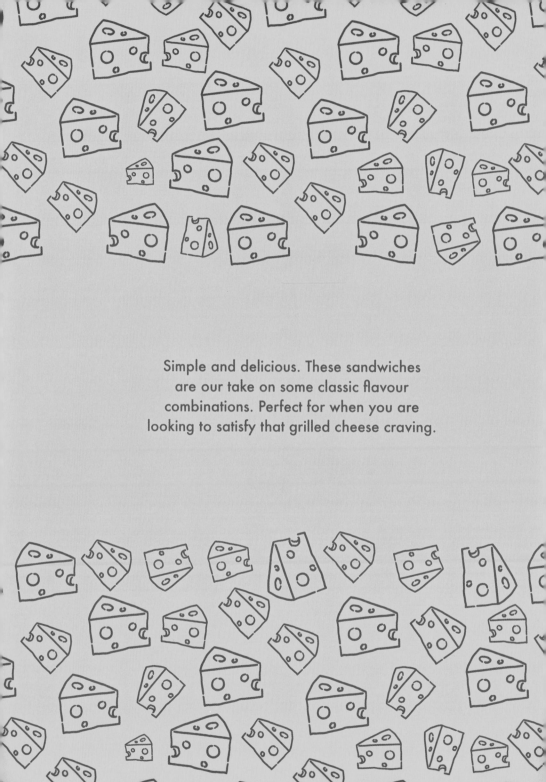

Simple and delicious. These sandwiches
are our take on some classic flavour
combinations. Perfect for when you are
looking to satisfy that grilled cheese craving.

EASY CHEESY

GMC

This is our take on the perfect grilled cheese. Feel free to mix it up
with your favourite cheeses as mentioned in the cheese low-down (see
page 14) but make sure they have great flavour, melt and stretch.
We love to eat this with pickles on the side but it's equally delicious
dipped in tomato soup or eaten under a duvet on a cold winter's day.

Serves 1

2 slices of sourdough bread,
  buttered on one side
150g (5¼oz) mixed grated
  cheese (see page 17 for
  our blend)
Generous 2 tbsp béchamel
  (see page 130)

Place the bread slices buttered side down. Sprinkle the
grated cheese evenly onto one slice of the bread and
spread an even layer of béchamel on the other slice.
Close the sandwich and cook using your preferred
method (see page 18).

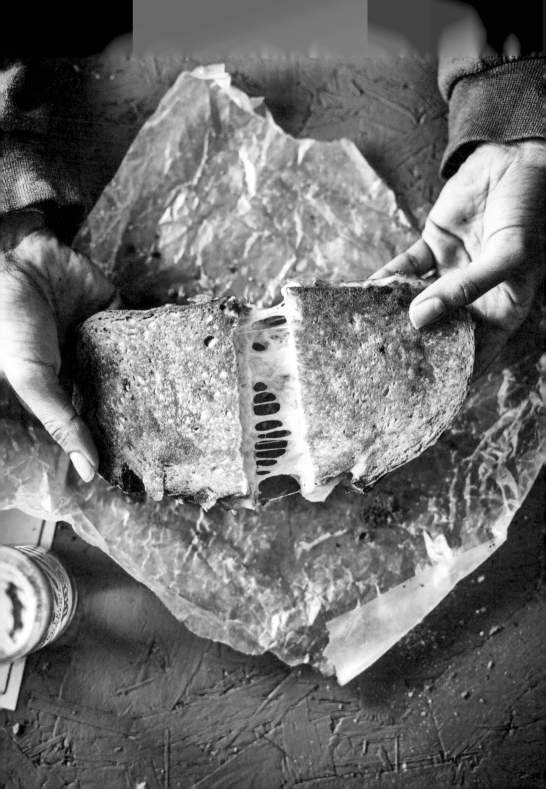

SPINACH, RICOTTA & PINE NUT

We both LOVE pasta and one of our favourites has to be spinach and ricotta cannelloni. This is our grilled cheese version and it works so well. It's a comforting classic with a lemony, peppery cheesy hit, perfect for a spring al fresco lunch or dinner.

Serves 1

2 rashers (slices) of smoked (lean) streaky bacon (optional)
2 slices of sourdough bread, buttered on one side
100g (3½oz) mixed grated cheese (see page 17 for our blend)
1 tbsp pine nuts, toasted

For the ricotta filling

200g (7oz) baby leaf spinach
250g (1 cup) ricotta
1 small garlic clove, grated
Finely grated zest and juice of 1 lemon
Salt and freshly ground pepper
75g (1 cup) freshly grated Parmesan

If you are including the bacon, grill or fry it until nice and crispy. Set aside.

For the ricotta filling, place the spinach in a bowl, pour over boiling water to cover and leave for 5 minutes to wilt before draining. Squeeze out the excess water and finely chop. Put the ricotta in a clean, dry bowl and add the garlic, lemon zest and juice. Season well (go heavy on the pepper) and mix in the chopped spinach and grated Parmesan.

Place the bread slices buttered side down and sprinkle the grated cheese over one slice. Spread the ricotta filling onto the other slice, add the crispy bacon, if using, and top with the toasted pine nuts. Close the sandwich and cook using your preferred method (see page 18).

WHAT'S POPPIN'

A firm favourite of ours with the cream cheese adding an indulgent element to this toastie. It came about from our love of jalapeño poppers (cheese-stuffed, fried chillies), which are cheesy and creamy with a touch of heat. We've added apricots to give a hint of sweetness. This relish recipe will make enough to fill a large jar, but will keep in the refrigerator for up to 2 weeks. It also works really well on a hot dog or as an accompaniment at a barbecue.

Serves 1

2 rashers (slices) of smoked streaky (lean) bacon (optional)
2 slices of sourdough bread, buttered on one side
100g (3½oz) mixed grated cheese (see page 17 for our blend)
2 tbsp cream cheese

For the relish
1 red (bell) pepper
1 green (bell) pepper
1 yellow (bell) pepper
100g (3½oz) dried soft apricots
85g (3oz) green jalapeño chillies, plus 3 tbsp brine from the jar
Juice of 1 lime
Pinch of salt

To make the relish, halve, deseed and finely dice all the (bell) peppers; set aside in a mixing bowl. Put the apricots in a food processor and add the chillies with the brine. Blitz to a paste and add to the mixing bowl. Add the lime juice and stir to combine. Add the salt and leave to rest for at least 1 hour.

For the toastie, if you are including the bacon, grill or fry it until nice and crispy.

Place the bread slices buttered side down and sprinkle the grated cheese over one slice. Spread the cream cheese onto the other slice, followed by an even layer of the relish on top. Add the crispy bacon, if using, before closing the sandwich and cooking using your preferred method (see page 18).

See next page for photographs

HEY PESTO

This is your typical Caprese sandwich. We use walnuts instead of pine nuts in our pesto to get a more rounded flavour and nutty texture. It is perfect on a sunny day served with a cold glass of white wine.

Serves 1

2 rashers (slices) of smoked streaky (lean) bacon (optional)
2 slices of sourdough bread, buttered on one side
100g (3½oz) mixed grated cheese (see page 17 for our blend)
50g (1¾oz) drained buffalo mozzarella, finely sliced
½ vine tomato, finely sliced
2 tbsp lemon, basil & walnut pesto (see page 134)

If you are including the bacon, grill or fry it until nice and crispy.

Place the bread slices buttered side down. Sprinkle the grated cheese evenly onto one slice of the bread, then add the mozzarella and tomato. Top with the bacon, if using, and drizzle the pesto on the other slice of bread. Close the sandwich and cook using your preferred method (see page 18).

PATTY MELT

This sandwich requires a little more time than our other quick, put-together combinations, but we can't tell you how much it's worth it. A patty melt is incredibly popular in the USA. It's essentially a burger inside a grilled cheese. The double cheese you get around the burger is just magical, and combined with our slow-roasted tomato ketchup it will instantly transport you to your happy place. We recommend you use the best meat you can afford, preferably aged. We use a 45-day-aged mix of chuck and short rib, with a fat content of around 30%. This sounds a little high, but it's what flavours the burgers and keeps them juicy.

Serves 2

4 slices of sourdough bread, buttered on one side
300g (10½oz) mixed grated cheese (see page 17 for our blend)
4 tbsp slow-roasted tomato ketchup (see page 131)

For the caramelized onion
1 tbsp rapeseed (canola) or other vegetable oil
1 white onion, finely chopped
½ tsp salt

For the burgers
280g (10oz) minced (ground) beef
1 tsp salt mixed with 1 tsp freshly ground pepper

Start by caramelizing the onion: heat the oil in a heavy, cast-iron frying pan over a medium heat, add the onion and fry, for about 10 minutes, until nicely softened and golden brown. Add the salt, mix well and transfer to a bowl.

For the burgers, wipe down the pan used for the onion and set over a medium-high heat. With your hands, form the minced (ground) beef into two patties, roughly the shape of the bread slices and at least 1cm (⅜-inch) thick. Add to the hot pan, sprinkle both with half the salt and pepper mixture and cook for 90 seconds (for medium). Flip over and sprinkle with the remaining seasoning and cook for another 90 seconds. For well done, cook for 2 minutes each side. As they cook, press them down with a spatula to form a good crust. They may smoke slightly, but don't worry! Remove the cooked burgers to a plate.

Place the bread slices buttered side down. Sprinkle 100g (3½oz) of the grated cheese over each of two of the slices. Top with 1 tablespoon of the caramelized onion followed by the burger and the remaining cheese. Spread 2 tablespoons slow-roasted tomato ketchup onto the other slices of bread before closing. Cook using your preferred method (see page 18). Be careful not to squish them down too much as they will start to fall apart.

Cut in half to see the glorious double cheese encased burger you have created.

See next page for photographs

RED PEPPER PESTO

Sweet, smoky and slightly spicy, this pesto has all the flavour of a spicy 'nduja sausage while being 100% vegetarian. Carnivores fret not, crispy bacon optional as always.

Serves 1

2 rashers (slices) of smoked streaky (lean) bacon (optional)
2 slices of sourdough bread, buttered on one side
100g (3½oz) mixed grated cheese (see page 17 for our blend)
2 tbsp cream cheese
2 tbsp red pepper pesto (see page 135)
Handful of baby spinach, washed and dried

If you are including the bacon, grill or fry it until nice and crispy.

Place the bread slices buttered side down and sprinkle the grated cheese evenly over one slice. Spread the cream cheese on the other slice, drizzle the pesto on top followed by the baby spinach. Add the bacon, if using, and close the sandwich before cooking using your preferred method (see page 18).

VEGGIE NUT CRUNCH

Autumn days call for a classic combination of sweet roasted veg, tangy goat's cheese and toasted nuts. The drizzle of honey goes really well with the goat's cheese, and makes this toastie an indulgent treat.

Serves 1

2 slices of sourdough bread, buttered on one side
100g (3½oz) mixed grated cheese (see page 17 for our blend)
40g (1½oz) goat's cheese log
Small handful of toasted chopped hazelnuts
1 tsp honey

For the roasted veg

2 red (bell) peppers, deseeded and cut into rough cubes
1 courgette (zucchini), cut into chunks
1 red onion, peeled and cut into chunks
½ tsp salt
½ tsp freshly ground pepper
3 tbsp olive oil

Preheat your oven to 220°C/425°F/Gas 7.

Add the chopped (bell) peppers, courgette (zucchini) and onion to a baking tray and spread out evenly. Sprinkle over the salt and pepper and drizzle over the oil. Mix well and roast in the oven for 40 minutes, giving the tray a shake now and again. Remove and set aside.

Place the bread slices buttered side down. Sprinkle the grated cheese evenly over one slice, followed by 3 tablespoons of the roasted veg mixture (save any left over for another time or use). Crumble over the goat's cheese, sprinkle over the toasted chopped hazelnuts and drizzle over the honey. Close the sandwich and cook using your preferred method (see page 18).

JUSTIN BRIEBER

The name that gets all the attention! This sandwich is a real British classic, and perfect for the morning after a big night out. We have given you our version but feel free to mix it up a bit or add some of our red onion confit (see page 137), fresh tomatoes or rocket (arugula), for extra flavour.

Serves 1

2 rashers (slices) of smoked streaky (lean) bacon
2 slices of sourdough bread, buttered on one side
100g (3½oz) mixed grated cheese (see page 17 for our blend)
50g (1¾oz) Brie, sliced

Grill or fry the bacon until nice and crispy. Place the bread slices buttered side down and sprinkle the grated cheese onto one slice, followed by the sliced Brie and crispy bacon. If you do want to add any onion confit or additionals (see introduction), do so now. Otherwise, close the sandwich and cook using your preferred method (see page 18).

NA'CHO CHEESE

We love the combination of a fresh salsa with a hint of chilli alongside melted cheese. It might seem like a strange addition but the corn chips really make this a winning sandwich. You can also add some more fire to yours at home by adding some Mexicana cheese to the blend.

Serves 4

8 slices of sourdough bread, buttered on one side
400g (14oz) mixed grated cheese (see page 17 for our blend, replacing 100g (3½oz) of the Cheddar with Mexicana, if desired)
4 handfuls of crushed tortilla chips
4 tbsp soured cream

For the salsa

2 vine tomatoes, finely diced
1 small red onion, finely diced
1 small green chilli, or to taste, finely diced (seeds left in for extra heat if you like)
Juice of 1 lime
Pinch of salt

To make the salsa, put the diced tomatoes, onion and chilli in a mixing bowl. Add the lime juice and salt, mix well and set aside. You can make this up to 2 hours in advance, but the fresher the better!

Place the bread slices buttered side down and sprinkle the grated cheese evenly onto four of the slices. Add a generous tablespoon of the salsa to each, followed by a handful of crushed tortilla chips. Spread the soured cream onto the remaining slices of bread and close the sandwiches before cooking using your preferred method (see page 18).

GRILLY CHEESE STEAK

If you have ever had a Philly cheesesteak then you will know it is one of the greatest sandwiches! Thin slices of beef with onions and peppers topped with melted cheese in a sub, better known as hoagie roll in the USA. We wanted to recreate a cheese toastie version that had all the flavour but avoided using cheese in a can (think Cheez Whiz/Velveeta).

Serves 2

2 tbsp olive oil
½ white onion, finely sliced
1 green (bell) pepper, deseeded and finely sliced
100g (3½oz) mushrooms, finely sliced
Salt and freshly ground pepper
200g (7oz) bavette/rib-eye steak, cut into thin strips
4 slices of sourdough bread, buttered on one side
200g (7oz) mixed grated cheese (see page 17 for our blend)

Heat the oil in a large frying pan over a medium heat and add the onion. Cook for 5 minutes then add the green (bell) pepper. Cook for 3–5 minutes until softened, add the mushrooms and season well with salt and pepper. Transfer the mixture to a mixing bowl and return the pan to a high heat. Add the steak strips and flash-fry for 2 minutes. Season and combine with the vegetables.

Place the bread slices buttered side down and top two slices with 75g (2¾oz) grated cheese each. Add the steak and vegetable mixture, followed by the rest of the cheese. Close the sandwiches and cook using your preferred method (see page 18).

See next page for photographs

FRESH TUNA MELT

We wanted to give the classic tuna melt an upgrade, taking it to the next level using rocket (arugula) and wasabi. It's the best version we've ever had.

Serves 2

2 x 120g (4¼oz) fresh tuna fillets
Olive oil, for rubbing
Salt and freshly ground pepper
4 slices of sourdough bread, buttered on one side
200g (7oz) mixed grated cheese (see page 17 for our blend)
2 tbsp wasabi mayonnaise
1 tbsp capers
4 gherkins, sliced
2 tsp finely diced onion
Couple of handfuls of rocket (arugula)

Rub the tuna with oil and heat a griddle pan over a high heat. When the pan is smoking hot, add the tuna and sear for 1 minute on each side. Remove from the pan, season to taste and set aside to rest and cool slightly before cutting into slices 4mm (⅛ inch) thick; it should be nice and pink in the middle.

Place the bread slices buttered side down and sprinkle the grated cheese evenly over two of the slices, followed by the sliced tuna. Spread the wasabi mayonnaise onto the other two slices. Divide the capers, sliced gherkins and diced onion between each, finishing with some rocket (arugula). Close the sandwiches and toast using your preferred method (see page 18).

ROASTED MUSHROOM

Roasting mushrooms gives them a great, meaty texture
that is perfect for this toastie. This takes more time,
but – trust us – the flavour is far more intense.

Serves 1

100g (3½oz) chestnut
(cremini) mushrooms,
quartered
1 garlic clove, finely chopped
1 tsp olive oil
Salt and freshly ground
pepper
2 slices of sourdough bread,
buttered on one side
100g (3½oz) mixed grated
cheese (see page 17 for
our blend)
Handful of fresh parsley,
leaves picked and finely
chopped

Preheat the oven to 200°C/400°F/Gas 6. Put the
quartered mushrooms in a roasting dish with the garlic
and olive oil. Season with salt and pepper to taste, mix
to coat and roast in the oven for 20 minutes, giving
them a little shake halfway through. Remove from the
oven and leave to cool slightly.

Place the bread slices buttered side down and
sprinkle the grated cheese over one slice, followed
by 1½ tablespoons of the mushrooms; there should
be enough to cover the bread and ensure you get
mushroom in every bite (save any left over for another
use). Add parsley before closing the sandwich and
cooking using your preferred method (see page 18).

MARINATED COURGETTE &
GOAT'S CHEESE

Light and full of freshness, this sandwich is perfect for a sunny day. The mint and chilli really lift the toastie to the next level. Leave the seeds in the chilli for extra heat.

Serves 2

4 slices of sourdough bread, buttered on one side
200g (7oz) mixed grated cheese (see page 17 for our blend)
80g (2¾oz) fresh goat's cheese

For the marinated courgette (zucchini)

1 courgette (zucchini)
½ red chilli, deseeded (optional) and finely chopped
8 fresh mint leaves, finely sliced
Finely grated zest and juice of ½ lemon
1 tbsp olive oil

Slice the courgette (zucchini) lengthways into 3–4mm (about ⅛-inch) slices and place in a bowl. Add the chilli, mint and lemon zest and juice. Drizzle over the oil, mix well, cover and refrigerate for at least 1 hour.

Heat a griddle pan to a medium heat and add the courgette slices, in batches if necessary. Cook for about 3 minutes on each side, until tender and marked with griddle lines.

Place the bread slices buttered side down. Sprinkle the grated cheese evenly over two of the slices and divide the griddled courgette slices over the top. Crumble the goat's cheese on top, close the sandwiches and cook using your preferred method (see page 18).

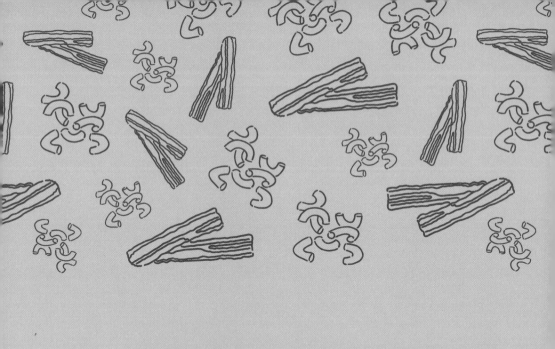

Famous in their own right. Put these on centre
stage for your friends and family.
We guarantee they won't be one hit wonders.

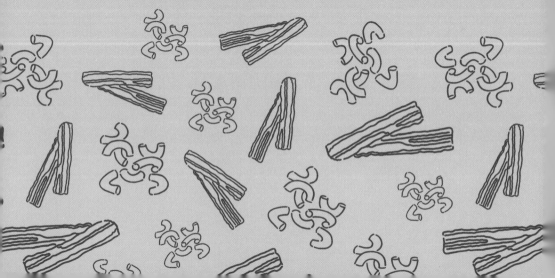

GRATEST
HITS

BABY GOT MAC

The sandwich that has been with us from the beginning, and continues to be the bestseller no matter where we go. Who knew mac 'n' cheese inside a sandwich would be such a hit? Without the pork and with added béchamel, this is also the basis of the mac 'n' cheese toastie on our stall, the Mac Attack.

For each sandwich
2 slices of sourdough bread, buttered on one side
150g (5¼oz) mixed grated cheese (see page 17 for our blend)
2 tbsp BBQ sauce (see page 130)

For the pulled pork (makes enough for 20 sandwiches)
2kg (4½ lb) pork shoulder, skin removed, deboned, fat scored and rolled (ask your butcher to do this)
2 tbsp paprika
2 tbsp brown sugar
2 tbsp salt
1 tbsp garlic powder
1 tbsp onion powder
1 tbsp ground black pepper
1 tsp mustard powder
½ tsp cayenne pepper
½ tsp ground coriander
½ tsp ground cumin

For the mac 'n' cheese (makes enough for 8 sandwiches)
500g (4 cups) macaroni
1 tsp salt
2 tbsp salted butter
100g (1 cup minus 2 tbsp) grated mozzarella
100g (1 packed cup plus 2 tbsp) grated Cheddar
100g (½ cup minus 1 tbsp) cream cheese

Put the pork shoulder in a baking tray. Mix all the dry ingredients together in a bowl then rub all over the pork, really massaging it in. Cover and refrigerate overnight.

Take the pork out of the refrigerator an hour before you want to cook it, and preheat the oven to 180°C/350°F/Gas 4. Cover with foil and put in the oven before reducing the oven temperature to 170°C/330°F/Gas 3. Cook for 5 hours, until the meat is falling apart (a temperature probe should read over 90°C/194°F). Leave to rest, covered, for 30 minutes, then remove any gristle and excess fat. Shred the meat, using either bear claws or 2 forks.

For the mac 'n' cheese, set the oven temperature to 190°C/375°F/Gas 5. Cook the macaroni in boiling salty water, for about 6–8 minutes, until al dente. Drain, reserving the cooking water. Place the macaroni in a baking dish, add the butter and all the cheeses. Slowly add enough of the reserved cooking water (about 90ml/6 tablespoons) to bring everything together until fully combined (the cheese should melt with the hot cooking water). Bake for about 15 minutes, until oozy but not golden. Leave to cool, then using your hands, separate it to break it up.

To assemble each sandwich, place the bread slices buttered down and sprinkle 100g (3½oz) of the grated cheese evenly over one slice. Add a big handful of the mac 'n' cheese, followed by the pulled pork. Spoon over the BBQ sauce and top with the remaining 50g (1¾oz) cheese. Close the sandwich and cook using your preferred method (see page 18).

KIM CANDASHIAN

This, and Confit West (page 55) were thought of in the same day, and that's why the names work so perfectly together. The candy bacon butter is rich, sweet and salty and works really well spread directly on toast or stirred through scrambled eggs. Guaranteed booty enhancer.

Serves 1

2 slices of sourdough bread, buttered on one side
100g (3½oz) mixed grated cheese (see page 17 for our blend)
½ vine tomato, sliced
Handful of rocket (arugula)
2 tbsp candy bacon butter (see page 133)

Place the bread slices buttered side down. Sprinkle the grated cheese evenly onto one slice of bread. Place the sliced tomato on top, then the rocket (arugula). Spread the candy bacon butter on the other slice of bread. Close the sandwich and cook using your preferred method (see page 18).

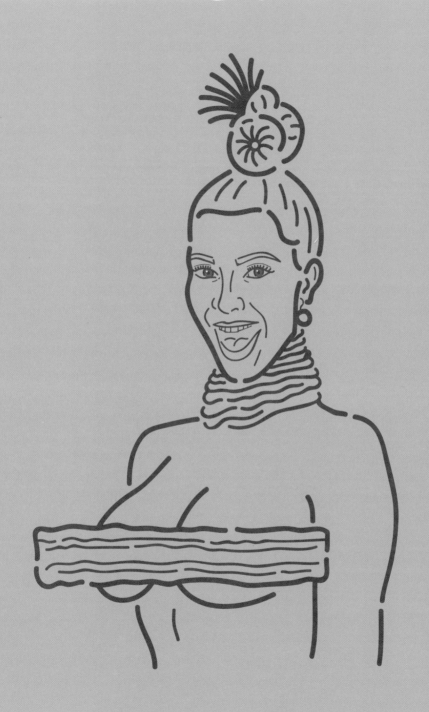

CONFIT WEST

Like the infamous rapper himself,
this sandwich will be sure to steal the limelight.

Serves 1

2 slices of sourdough bread,
  buttered on one side
100g (3½oz) mixed grated
  cheese (see page 17 for
  our blend)
Handful of rocket (arugula)
2 tbsp red onion confit (see
  page 137)

Place the bread slices buttered side down. Sprinkle the grated cheese evenly onto one slice of bread and top with the rocket (arugula). Spread the red onion confit on the other slice of bread. Close the sandwich and cook using your preferred method (see page 18).

GHOSTIE

This was a sandwich we came up with for a Halloween special. The beetroot (beet) was a given because of its deep bloody red colour. We pickled it to give it extra zing! Goat's cheese and chives are a classic combination that work really well with the earthiness of the beetroot.

Serves 1

2 slices of sourdough bread, buttered on one side
150g (5¼oz) soft goat's cheese
1 tsp finely chopped chives

For the pickled beetroot (beet)

3–4 medium, raw beetroot (beet)
2 tbsp olive oil
200g (1 cup) caster (superfine) sugar
300ml (1¼ cups) white wine vinegar
2 tbsp balsamic vinegar
200ml (1 cup minus 3 tbsp) water
2 bay leaves

Preheat the oven to 180°C/350°F/Gas 4. Trim any leaves or stalks off the beetroot (beet), clean and coat in 1 tablespoon of the oil. Wrap in foil and roast in the oven for 1–1½ hours, until the point of a knife can be easily inserted. Remove and leave to cool in the foil, then unwrap and peel off the skin; use gloves or paper towels to stop your hands being stained. Cut into thick slices and place in a sterilized jar.

For the pickling liquor, put the sugar, both vinegars, water and bay leaves in a saucepan and bring to the boil. Turn down to a simmer and gently stir so that all the sugar is dissolved. Carefully pour enough of the hot liquid into the jar to fully cover the beetroot (depending on the size of the jar, you may not need it all). Leave to cool, uncovered, then spoon the remaining tablespoon of oil into the jar and seal. Leave for at least 24 hours, and store in the refrigerator for up to a month.

To assemble the sandwich, place the bread slices buttered side down. Spread the goat's cheese onto one slice of the bread. Place some of the pickled beetroot slices on top, then sprinkle on the chives. Close the sandwich and cook using your preferred method (see page 18).

CHILLENA GOMEZ

One of our more recent creations but already a firm favourite on the stall.
It's not a conventional chilli, as neither of us like beans in ours,
but feel free to throw them in if you want to serve in a bowl rather
than a sandwich (in which case these quantities will serve 4).

For each sandwich
2 slices of sourdough bread,
  buttered on one side
100g (3½oz) mixed grated
  cheese (see page 17 for
  our blend)
2 tbsp soured cream
1 green chilli, sliced

For the chilli (serves 6)
Olive oil, for cooking
500g (1lb 2oz) minced
  (ground) beef
1 onion, chopped
3 garlic cloves, very finely
  chopped
1 tsp chilli powder
1 tsp ground cumin
½ tsp smoked paprika
¼ tsp cayenne pepper
½ tsp ground chipotle chilli
½ x 400g (14oz) can
  chopped tomatoes
500ml (generous 2 cups)
  good beef stock
1 tsp dried oregano
1 tsp brown sugar
1 tsp salt

Heat a tablespoon of oil in a saucepan, add the
minced (ground) beef and fry, stirring, until golden
brown, about 8–10 minutes. Remove to a bowl;
there should be some fat left in the pan. If not, add a
tablespoon of oil. Place back over the heat, add the
onion and cook for 6–8 minutes until golden and tender.
Add the garlic and cook for a further minute. Add the
chilli powder, cumin, smoked paprika, cayenne and
chipotle chilli. Stir together, then add the beef back in.
Add the chopped tomatoes, stock, oregano and sugar.

Bring to the boil, then reduce to a simmer and cook
for about 40 minutes, stirring occasionally and adding
water if necessary. Once reduced, stir in the salt. You
should have a rich chilli.

Place the bread slices buttered side down. Sprinkle
the grated cheese evenly onto one slice followed by
2–3 tablespoons of the cooked chilli mixture. Top with
the soured cream and sliced green chilli. Close and
cook using your preferred method (see page 18).

This sandwich can get messy, but in a good way.
Prepare to lick your fingers clean.

CHERRY MAGUIRE

This cherry cola short rib is the business! It is rich, sweet and sticky and works perfectly with cheese to create a toastie that will complete you. It's also great on its own with a side of mash and buttered greens.

For each sandwich

2 slices of sourdough bread, buttered on one side
150g (5¼oz) mixed grated cheese (see page 17 for our blend)

For the cherry cola short rib (serves 6–8)

1.5kg (3 lb 3oz) beef short ribs, trimmed
Salt and freshly ground pepper
2 tbsp vegetable oil
2 medium onions, sliced
2 garlic cloves, crushed
1 litre (4½ cups) beef stock
330ml (1⅜ cups) cherryade (not the no-added-sugar kind)
330ml (1⅜ cups) cola
240ml (1 cup) tomato ketchup
3 tbsp brown sugar

Preheat the oven to 150°C/300°F/Gas 2. Season the short ribs with salt and pepper. Heat 1 tablespoon of the oil in a frying pan over a high heat, add the ribs and sear for 2–3 minutes on each side, until evenly browned. Remove from the pan and set aside in a roasting dish or tin. Return the frying pan to a medium heat and add the remaining tablespoon of oil and the onions. Allow to soften slightly before adding the garlic and cooking for another 5 minutes. Transfer to the roasting dish, then deglaze the pan with some of the beef stock and add to the roasting dish, along with the rest of the stock. Cover the dish in foil and cook for 4 hours. Remove from the oven, take the short ribs out of the juices and set aside to rest.

Strain the meat juices into a saucepan and skim as much of the fat as you can off the surface (you can leave it to cool at this point, which will make it easier). Place the pan over a high heat and add the cherryade, cola, ketchup and sugar. Bring to a boil and leave to simmer over a medium heat for 30–45 minutes, stirring every 10 minutes or so, until reduced and thickened.

While the sauce is reducing, remove the bones from the ribs, as well as any gristle. Using 2 forks, shred the meat. When the sauce is ready, pour it over the shredded meat.

To assemble each sandwich, place the bread slices buttered side down and sprinkle 100g (3½oz) of the grated cheese evenly over one slice. Spread 2 tablespoons of the short rib evenly onto the other slice of the bread and top with the remaining 50g (1¾oz) cheese. Close the sandwich and cook using your preferred method (see page 18).

EVERY DAY
I'M TRUFFLIN'

Perfect for autumn days when you just need some 'me' time. Roasting a whole butternut yields quite a lot but you can use the rest up in a salad bowl, or even blitz with some stock to make a great soup.

Serves 1

2 slices of sourdough bread, buttered on one side
100g (3½oz) mixed grated cheese (see page 17 for our blend)
3–4 tsp ricotta
1 tsp truffle oil

For the squash and onions

1 medium butternut squash
8 sage leaves
Olive oil, for roasting
Salt and freshly ground pepper
1 red onion, sliced

Preheat the oven to 180°C/350°F/Gas 4. Peel, halve and deseed the butternut squash, then cut into slices about 4mm (⅛ inch) thick. Place in a roasting dish along with the sage leaves, a drizzle of olive oil and salt and pepper to taste. Rub the whole lot together so the squash slices are well covered and roast for 30 minutes, until tender.

Meanwhile, put the sliced onion in a small roasting dish with enough oil to cover (about 1 tablespoon) and some salt and pepper. Roast in the oven alongside the squash for about 20 minutes, until softened and browned. Remove and leave to cool slightly.

Place the bread slices buttered side down and sprinkle the grated cheese over one slice, followed by a few slices of squash and 1 teaspoon of the roasted onion. Using a teaspoon, place a few dollops of ricotta on top before drizzling over the truffle oil. Close the sandwich and cook using your preferred method (see page 18).

JAY CHEESE & BEAN-ONCÉ

The inspiration for this sandwich came as we were driving home in the van one Sunday afternoon. Cheese and beans are so good together, it just made sense to put them in a sandwich. Baked beans are a comforting classic and our homemade version is great on toast or jacket potatoes. The beans will warm you from the inside out. Double the recipe and eat them later in the week.

For each sandwich
2 chipolata sausages
2 slices of sourdough bread, buttered on one side
100g (3½oz) mixed grated cheese (see page 17 for our blend)

For the baked beans (serves 4–6)
2 tbsp olive oil
1 red onion, finely chopped
2 garlic cloves, very finely chopped
2 x 300g (10½oz) cans haricot beans, drained and rinsed
1 x 400g (14oz) can chopped tomatoes
1 tbsp dark muscovado sugar
2 tbsp cider vinegar
500ml (generous 2 cups) water
Salt and freshly ground pepper

Heat the oil for the beans in a pan over a medium heat, add the onion and cook until slightly browned and caramelized. This can take up to 10 minutes. Add the garlic and let it cook out for 1–2 minutes. Add the drained beans, tomatoes, sugar, cider vinegar and water, reduce the heat and simmer for 20–30 minutes, stirring occasionally, until the sauce is rich and coats the beans. Season with salt and pepper to taste. If not using straight away, leave to cool then store in an airtight container in the refrigerator for up to 3 days.

Grill the sausages until cooked, then leave to cool slightly before cutting them in half lengthways.

To assemble each sandwich, place the bread slices buttered side down. Sprinkle the grated cheese evenly onto one slice and add 2 generous tablespoons of the baked beans. Top with the 4 slices of sausage. Close the sandwich and cook using your preferred method (see page 18).

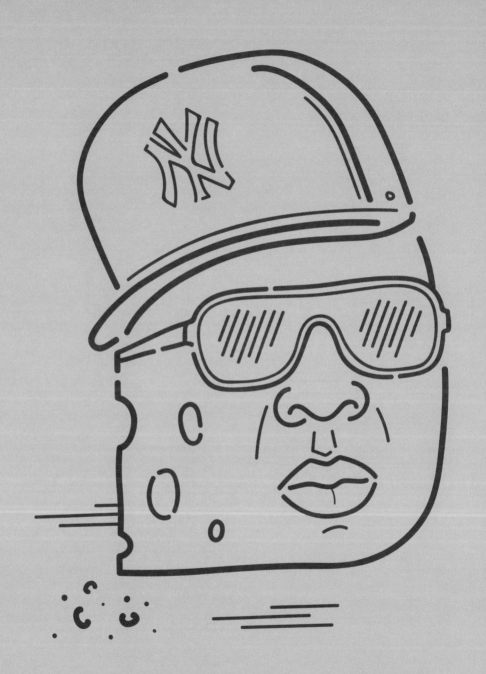

Rainbows, doughnuts and Frazzles. Life is short, have a bit of fun. These are our more unique combinations. Bound to go down in history.

LEGENDAIRIES

RAINBOW TOASTIE

We first saw the rainbow grilled cheese being made by the Kala Café in Hong Kong in 2016. Our third birthday was coming up and we thought it would be a fun idea to recreate it. We knew if we were going to do this, as well as looking pretty, it had to be truly delicious. Beetroot (beet) was a great starting point, given its bright colour. From there, we tried out a few complementing combinations before we got to our dream sandwich.

Serves 4

1 red onion, roughly chopped
4 tbsp olive oil
About 2 small dabs of blue food colouring gel
600g (1lb 5oz) mixed grated cheese (see page 17 for our blend)
50g (1¾oz) cooked beetroot (beet)
100g (3½oz) rocket (arugula)
8 slices of sourdough bread, buttered on one side
200g (7oz) fresh goat's cheese
Truffle oil, for drizzling

Preheat the oven to 200°C/400°F/Gas 6.

For the blue, toss the onion in 1 tablespoon of the olive oil and spread out on a baking tray. Roast in the oven for 20–30 minutes, until softened, then remove and leave to cool before blending to a fine purée. Add the blue food colouring and mix well. Combine with 200g (7oz) of the grated cheese mixture.

For the pink, process the beetroot (beet) to a purée using a blender. Transfer to a bowl and mix in 200g (7oz) of the remaining grated cheese mixture.

For the green, blend together the rocket (arugula) and the remaining 3 tablespoons olive oil until it reaches a fine paste consistency. Mix well into the remaining 200g (7oz) of the grated cheese mixture.

To assemble the sandwiches, place the bread slices buttered side down, so that they are vertical to you. Add the three coloured mixtures, in equal segments, down the long end of one slice. Start with the pink, then blue and finally the green (to get the best effect).

Break up the goat's cheese and divide between each topped bread slice. Drizzle with a little truffle oil, close the sandwiches and cook using your preferred method (see page 18).

Leave the cooked sandwiches to sit for about 30 seconds before slicing each in half. Camera phones at the ready!

See page 4 for photograph

PB&J

Possibly one of the stranger combinations we have done, but if you love peanut butter, it's the one for you. It is sweet, savoury, rich and cheesy all at the same time and a personal favourite of ours. This makes much more peanut butter and American cheese than you need for a single sandwich, but both store well.

Serves 1

2 rashers (slices) of smoked streaky (lean) bacon (optional)
2 slices of sourdough bread, buttered on one side
2 tbsp red chilli jam

For the peanut butter
500g (3¾ cups) blanched raw peanuts

For the American cheese
1 tbsp water
1½ tsp vegetarian gelatine powder
350g (12½oz) mixed grated cheese (we use our cheese blend on page 17, but including some red Leicester will give you the yellow colour more reminiscent of American cheese)
1 tbsp whole milk powder
1 tsp salt
⅛ tsp cream of tartar
150ml (10 tbsp) whole milk

Preheat the oven to 180°C/350°F/Gas 4. Spread the peanuts on a baking tray and bake in the oven for 15 minutes, tossing every 5 minutes, until golden brown. Remove and set aside to cool, then blend until smooth in a powerful blender. Store in a sterilized jar for up to 4 weeks.

For the American cheese, line a loaf tin with cling film. Be sure to leave enough excess hanging over the sides to be able to go all the way over the top again. Put the water in a small bowl, sprinkle the gelatine over it and leave for a few minutes to soften. In a food processor, pulse together the grated cheese, milk powder, salt and cream of tartar to combine. Bring the milk to the boil in a small saucepan, remove from the heat and whisk in the gelatine mixture until completely dissolved. With the food processor running, slowly add the hot milk mixture until the cheese mixture is smooth; you may need to scrape down the sides a few times. Immediately transfer the cheese to the prepared tin and pack it down to remove any air pockets. Fold the cling film over the top and refrigerate for at least 3 hours. It can be stored in the refrigerator for up to 1 month, tightly wrapped.

For the sandwich, if you are including bacon, grill or fry until nice and crispy.

To assemble your sandwich, place the bread slices buttered side down. Spread 2 tablespoons of the peanut butter onto one slice. Slice 150g (5¼oz) of the American cheese and place on top, trying to cover most of the surface. Add your bacon, if using, and spread chilli jam onto the other slice. Close and cook using your preferred method (see page 18).

This makes for the perfect midnight snack.

See previous page for photographs

DOUGHNUT GRILLED CHEESE

Doughnuts are sweet. Should they be used in a grilled cheese sandwich recipe? Hell, yeah! Sounds odd, but have faith. We love sweet and salty combinations at Grill My Cheese, and we couldn't help but give this a go. The sweet glaze on the doughnut combined with the blue cheese and the hot sauce fills a massive craving you didn't even know you had. This is one that you will make on more than one occasion.

Serves 1

2 rashers (slices) of streaky (lean) bacon
1 plain glazed ring doughnut
1 slice of Mexicana cheese (chilli cheese)
1 slice of American cheese (see page 74 for homemade)
20g (¾oz) creamy blue cheese, such as Roquefort, crumbled
2 tsp hot sauce
3 slices of gherkin
Handful of salted matchstick crisps/fries

Grill or fry the bacon until crisp, then break up into pieces.

Slice the doughnut in half horizontally, so that you have two rings as the base of your sandwich. Place them glaze side down.

Place the Mexicana cheese slice on one of the rings and the American cheese slice on the other. On top of the smoked cheese add the bacon, blue cheese, hot sauce and gherkins. Top with the matchstick crisps/fries and close the sandwich. Cook in a dry frying pan over a low-medium heat (the glaze on the doughnut can cause it to burn quite quickly so be careful) until squished and caramelized, and the cheese is fully melted.

See next page for photographs

SLUMDOG GRILLIONAIRE

We both grew up eating a version of a 'Bombay sandwich' – leftover curry on white bread thrown into the Breville. Although very different to this, the concept is the same: spicy potato, chutney and cheese. We created our own version for Grill My Cheese. The spicy potato coupled with the fresh coriander (cilantro) chutney creates an explosion of flavours in the best possible way.

Serves 2

4 slices of sourdough bread, buttered on one side
200g (7oz) mixed grated cheese (see page 17 for our blend)
2 tbsp diced red onion
2 tbsp coriander, apple & peanut chutney (see page 136)

For the spiced potato

350g (12¼oz) potatoes, washed and unpeeled
1 garlic clove, crushed
1 thin green chilli, finely chopped
½ red chilli, finely chopped, or more to taste
¼ tsp ground turmeric
Juice of ½ lemon
Pinch of salt
½ tsp sugar

Boil the potatoes until tender, then drain and leave to cool slightly before removing the skin and mashing (you can also use a ricer or grater for this). Add the remaining ingredients and mix well to combine. Give it a taste and, depending on how spicy you like it, add some more chilli.

Place the bread slices buttered side down. Spread 2 tablespoons of the spiced potato evenly over two of the slices. Top with the grated cheese and diced onion before drizzling over the chutney. Close the sandwiches and cook using your preferred method (see page 18).

WHO WANTS TO BE

A GRILLIONAIRE?

PIZZA GRILLED CHEESE

We love traditional pizzas with sourdough bases cooked in wood-fired ovens but, when feeling low (or hungover), nothing quite beats a beautifully melty 'delivered to your door' pizza. This lives up to the filth factor: it's made on standard white bread and we include a Frazzle crust for added crunch! Mix up the toppings with your own selection. Just make sure you don't overfill the toastie, or it will fall apart.

Serves 1

3 slices of basic white bread, buttered on one side
1 slice of smoked Cheddar
2 tbsp ready-made pizza sauce (or the slow-roasted tomato ketchup on page 131)
2 slices of American cheese (see page 74 for homemade)
50g (scant ½ cup) grated mozzarella

For the toppings

1 tbsp sweetcorn
3 slices of pepperoni (optional)
5 jalapeño chillies from a jar, roughly chopped

For the Frazzle crust (optional)

2 handfuls of grated Cheddar
2 handful of crushed Frazzles (bacon corn snacks)

Place one slice of bread buttered side down. Lay the slice of smoked Cheddar on the bread, then 1 tablespoon of the pizza sauce. Scatter the sweetcorn on top then follow with another slice of bread.

On top of the second slice of bread, add the American cheese, a second tablespoon of pizza sauce, the pepperoni, if using, the grated mozzarella and the jalapeños. Finish with the third slice of bread, buttered side facing out.

If you are not including the Frazzle crust, simply cook using your preferred method (see page 18).

For the Frazzle crust, first cook the sandwich using the frying pan method on page 18. Once cooked, set the sandwich aside and place the pan back over a medium heat. Sprinkle in 1 handful of the grated Cheddar and, when it starts to bubble, add 1 handful of the crushed Frazzles and immediately add your closed sandwich to the pan. Press down with a spatula or heavy pan to ensure an even melt and leave to cook for 3–4 minutes before flipping and repeating on the other side, adding the remaining Cheddar and Frazzles to the pan before adding the turned sandwich, to achieve the crust on both sides. Cut and devour immediately. You won't regret it!

THANKSGRILLING

Our homage (or fromage) to the national holiday.
Having eaten our fair share of Thanksgiving dinners
with friends from across the pond, we tried to incorporate
the best bits in to this grilled cheese sandwich.

For each sandwich
2 slices of sourdough bread,
  buttered on one side
100g (3½oz) mixed grated
  cheese
6 green beans, cooked until
  tender then refreshed in iced
  water (to keep their colour)
2 slices of cornbread (see
  recipe opposite), cut 1cm
  (⅜ inch) thick

For the pulled turkey (makes enough for 4–6 sandwiches)
1 turkey leg
1 tsp salt
1 tsp freshly ground black
  pepper
1 red onion, roughly chopped
1 carrot, roughly chopped
1 celery stick, roughly
  chopped
3 garlic cloves, smashed
  (skin on)
1 sprig of rosemary
1 bay leaf
2 tbsp olive oil

For the gravy
2 tbsp plain (all-purpose) flour
300ml (1¼ cups) good-quality
  chicken stock
1 tsp salt
2 tbsp cranberry sauce

Preheat the oven to 180°C/350°F/Gas 4. Season the turkey with the salt and pepper. Spread the onion, carrot and celery out on a roasting tray, then add the garlic cloves, rosemary sprig and bay leaf. Drizzle with the oil and mix everything together. Put the turkey on top of the vegetables, cover with foil. Bake for 1 hour, remove and leave to rest for 20 minutes. Take the turkey out of the baking tray and remove any skin and gristle. Pull the meat away from the bone and shred using two forks.

Place the baking tray, with the remaining vegetables, over a medium heat. Cook for a few minutes, mashing everything together using the back of a wooden spoon or a fork. This provides the base for the gravy.

Gradually stir in the flour, so that it is fully incorporated, then slowly stir in the stock. Leave to simmer for 20–30 minutes, until thickened and reduced. Strain through a sieve and stir in the salt and cranberry sauce before dividing between two bowls. Add the pulled turkey to one bowl and mix to combine. (Leave the other half to act as a dipper/moistmaker.)

Increase the oven temperature to 200°C/400°F/Gas 6. Put the torn sourdough into a food processor and blitz to breadcrumbs. Add the remaining stuffing ingredients to the breadcrumbs and mix well. Spread out in a greased ovenproof dish and bake for 30 minutes until golden brown all over and cooked through. Leave to cool before removing and slicing.

To assemble each sandwich, place the bread slices buttered side down. Top one slice with most of the grated cheese (leave a sprinkling for the end) followed by a slice or two of stuffing (about 50g/1¾oz).

For the pork stuffing
1 slice of stale sourdough
  bread, roughly torn
1 large onion, chopped
2 garlic cloves, crushed
450g (15¾oz) finely minced
  pork (at least 20% fat) or
  sausage meat
1 tbsp freshly chopped
  parsley
2 tbsp freshly chopped sage
1 tsp salt
1 tsp freshly ground pepper
Vegetable oil, for greasing

Lay the green beans on top before adding 2 heaped tablespoons of the pulled turkey, and the slices of cornbread side by side. Drizzle over 2 tablespoons of gravy, top with the remaining cheese, close and cook using your preferred method (see page 18).

CORNBREAD

**Makes enough for
10 slices**
60ml (¼ cup) vegetable oil,
  plus extra for greasing
150g (1 cup) cornmeal
140g (1 cup) plain
  (all-purpose) flour
2 tbsp caster (superfine) sugar
2 tsp baking powder
¼ tsp bicarbonate of soda
  (baking soda)
½ tsp salt
240ml (1 cup) buttermilk
  (or milk)
2 eggs

Preheat the oven to 190°C/375°F/Gas 5. Lightly grease a 23 x 12cm/9 x 5-inch loaf tin.

Mix the dry ingredients together in a large bowl. Add the buttermilk or milk, oil and eggs and whisk to combine.

Pour the mixture into the prepared tin and bake for about 35 minutes, until a toothpick inserted into the centre comes out clean. Leave to cool a little before turning out of the tin, then leave to cool completely before slicing.

BUTTERMILK
MAC 'N' CHEESE PANCAKES

If it weren't already obvious, we love a bit of carb-on-carb action. The pancake batter has cooked macaroni in it as well as a generous amount of Cheddar. We serve ours with crispy bacon, hot sauce and maple syrup.

Serves 6 (makes about 12 pancakes)

200g (1½ cups) plain (all-purpose) flour
65g (½ cup) wholewheat flour
2 tsp baking powder
1 tbsp sugar
1 tsp salt
240ml (1 cup) whole milk
320ml (1¼ cups) buttermilk
2 eggs
2 tbsp butter, melted
300g (2½ cups) cooked macaroni
150g (1⅔ cups) grated Cheddar
Melted butter, for greasing

To serve (optional)
Crispy bacon
Maple syrup
Hot sauce

Whisk the dry ingredients together in a large bowl. In a separate bowl, whisk together the milk, buttermilk, eggs and melted butter. Add to the dry ingredients and stir until just combined (the batter will be slightly lumpy). Fold in the cooked macaroni and grated Cheddar.

Preheat and lightly grease a griddle or large frying pan over a medium heat. Spoon the batter onto the griddle, one ladleful at a time; it should spread into a pancake about 7cm (2¾ inches) in diameter. Cook until the underside is golden brown and slightly stiff, about 3–4 minutes. Flip and cook on the other side until golden brown. Repeat with the remaining batter and serve warm with crispy bacon, maple syrup and hot sauce, if you like.

Sugar and spice and all things nice.
No meal is complete without dessert.

BRIE
HAPPY

I BRIE-LIVE I CAN PIE

In the namesake land of American Pie, they make traditional apple pies with Cheddar crusts. So, using this idea as a starting point, we came up with this heavenly dessert creation.

Serves 1

25g (scant 2 tbsp) butter
1 tbsp brown sugar
½ tsp ground cinnamon
1 apple (Braeburn or Golden Delicious), cored and sliced about 2mm (1/16-inch) thick
2 slices of sourdough bread, buttered on one side
100g (3½oz) Brie, sliced
30g (1oz) Cheddar, grated

Melt the butter and sugar in a saucepan, then stir in the cinnamon. Add the apple slices and cook over a gentle heat for about 5 minutes. They should be softened slightly but still keep their shape and have a slight bite. Remove from the heat and spread out on a tray to stop them cooking further.

To assemble the sandwich, place the bread slices buttered side down. Lay the Brie slices on one slice of bread and top with the apples, spreading them out evenly. Add the grated Cheddar, close the sandwich and cook using your preferred method (see page 18).

BLUEBERRY COMPOTE &
ALMOND PRALINE

This was the first dessert toastie that we came up with. It may look like there are a lot of ingredients, but it's really easy and makes a great treat for friends and family. If you're making this just for yourself, you will be left with some compote and praline but both keep well – the compote for up to a week in the refrigerator, and the praline for three weeks in an airtight container. Serve with yoghurt and granola, porridge or over pancakes.

Serves 1

50g (¼ cup) cream cheese, softened
20g (2¾ tbsp) sifted icing (confectioners') sugar, plus extra to serve
2 slices of raisin bread, buttered on one side

For the blueberry compote

200g (generous 1½ cups) blueberries
50g (5¾ tbsp) icing (confectioners') sugar
½ tsp vanilla extract
Grated zest of 1 orange and juice of ½

For the almond praline

50g (⅔ cup) flaked (slivered) almonds
125g (⅔ cup) caster (superfine) sugar
Squeeze of lemon juice

For the compote, put the blueberries in a small pan with the icing (confectioners') sugar, vanilla extract, orange zest and juice. Place over a medium heat. The blueberries will burst and everything will start to get syrupy. Cook for 5 minutes before taking off the heat and leaving to cool.

For the praline, gently toast the flaked (slivered) almonds in a dry frying pan, then tip into a bowl and leave to cool. Add the sugar to the frying pan and cook, without stirring but giving the pan the odd shake, until melted and golden (it should reach 300°C/570°F on a sugar thermometer). Be careful as it will be extremely hot. Add the toasted almonds and lemon juice. Stir well and tip onto a silicone-lined baking sheet. Leave to cool.

Once cool, either smash to break up, or cut with a knife. It is great to eat as it is, but for the sandwich put some in a food processor and gently pulse; you get some chunks and sugary dust.

To assemble the sandwich, mix the cream cheese and icing sugar together in a bowl. Place the raisin bread buttered side down. Top one slice with the sweetened cream cheese, then 2 tablespoons of the blueberry compote and a handful of crushed almond praline.

Close the sandwich and cook over a gentle heat in a dry frying pan until golden on both sides. (This sandwich is a bit too delicate for a panini press.) Remove, sift ½ tablespoon of icing sugar over and serve.

See next page for photographs

MINCE PIE TOASTIE

This recipe came about on a cold and wet winter's day while trading on London's Southbank over Christmas. We love these sweet-savoury combinations and figured the rich fruit filling of a mince pie would work with a sharp Cheddar. Curious as ever, we tried it in a toastie. Best decision ever! The pastry adds a whole other element to the sandwich.

Serves 1

2 slices of sourdough bread, buttered on one side
75g (2¾oz) extra mature (sharp) hard cheese, grated
25g (1oz) cow's mozzarella, grated
2 mince pies

Place the bread slices buttered side down. Mix the grated cheeses together and sprinkle onto one of the slices. Add the mince pies and smash them slightly with the palm of your hand, so the cheese can melt evenly. Close the sandwich and cook using your preferred method (see page 18).

BLUE CHEESE, FIG & WALNUT

ICE CREAM SANDWICH

This is hands-down the best ice cream you will eat, FACT! It sounds strange, but trust us. Blue cheese can have a number of different flavour profiles. Given the combination we were going for in this ice cream with the rich, fudgy figs, it was important to find a cheese that carried notes of sweet caramel. We recommend using a Danish Blue – Castello is probably the easiest to find, but both the Creamy Blue and the Extra Creamy work well.

Serves 1

For each sandwich
1 brioche bun, cut in half horizontally, or 2 slices of brioche bread

For the ice cream (makes 900ml/3¾ cups)
180ml (¾ cup) double (heavy) cream
60ml (¼ cup) whole milk
2 egg yolks
1 tbsp brown sugar
125g (4½oz) blue cheese (see introduction)
120ml (½ cup) sweetened condensed milk
30g (⅓ cup) walnut halves
40g (⅓ cup) dried soft figs, cut into 4mm (⅛-inch) cubes

Warm the cream and milk together in a heavy pan over a low heat. Meanwhile, whisk the egg yolks with the sugar to incorporate. Slowly add the warmed milk and cream to the egg yolks, whisking constantly. Strain into a bowl and return to the pan over a gentle heat. Keep whisking until the custard thickens and coats the back of a spoon.

Take off the heat and crumble in the blue cheese, whisking until most of it has melted. Reserve some chunks to add in later (these give a real cheesy hit when you are eating it). Stir in the condensed milk and transfer the mixture to a bowl. Cool, then refrigerate to chill for 30–60 minutes.

While the mixture is cooling, preheat the oven to 170°C/330°F/Gas 3. Spread the walnuts out on a baking tray and toast for 10 minutes, keeping an eye on them to ensure they don't burn. Remove and leave to cool before roughly chopping.

Churn the chilled mixture in an ice cream machine according to the manufacturer's instructions. Once the mixture has thickened to a dropping consistency, add the walnuts and figs and churn until fully set. Add the reserved blue cheese and churn briefly to mix. Pop in the freezer until you are ready to eat, or devour immediately!

For the sandwich, toast the brioche under the grill or in the toaster. Add a generous dollop of ice cream. Close and enjoy.

MILKY WAY MELT

A very happy accident of ours, this toastie is a great way to use up the smaller ends of the bread when you buy a freeform loaf. Give it a try using your favourite chocolate bars.

Serves 1

2 slices of sourdough bread, buttered on one side
2 x Milky Way (3 Musketeers) bars

Place the bread slices buttered side down. Put the Milky Way (3 Musketeers) bars on one slice, side by side. Close the sandwich and cook on a medium heat using your preferred method (see page 18).

MASCARPONE SOFT SERVE

WITH A SELECTION OF TOPPINGS

This rich, creamy ice cream is so quick and easy to make. You can even prep everything in advance so all you have to do is blitz and pipe to serve. We have recommended a few toppings we love, but go crazy and experiment with whatever you like.

Makes 800ml (3⅓ cups)

340ml (scant 1½ cups) whole milk
120ml (½ cup) sweetened condensed milk
55g (scant ⅓ cup) caster (superfine) sugar
2½ tsp powdered gelatine
Pinch of salt
250g (1 cup plus 1½ tbsp) mascarpone

For the toppings

Sea salt and extra virgin olive oil
Balsamic reduction

Snickers sauce:

100ml (7 tbsp) double (heavy) cream
50g (1¾oz) dark (semisweet) chocolate, roughly chopped
50g (1¾oz) milk chocolate, roughly chopped
50g (1¾oz) smooth peanut butter (see page 74 for homemade)
2 tbsp golden (light corn) syrup

Whisk the milk, condensed milk and sugar together in a pan. Sprinkle the powdered gelatine and salt evenly on top, then bring to a simmer and whisk for a minute until the gelatine has fully dissolved. Remove from the heat and add the mascarpone, whisking to ensure it is lump-free. Pour the mixture into a shallow dish, leave to cool then freeze for 4–6 hours, until hardened. Score the mixture into small cubes with a knife, then freeze again for another 6 hours or overnight, or until needed (this can be made several days ahead).

For the Snickers sauce, combine the cream, both chocolates, peanut butter and syrup in a pan. Place over a low heat and stir until everything has melted together.

Remove the ice cream from the freezer and pulse in a food processor or blender to soften. If you are feeling fancy, put into a piping bag and pipe it to serve, or just dollop into bowls with one of the toppings.

Every Batman needs a Robin.
These sidekicks are the perfect
supporting act to all our superstars.

SIDES &
SMALL PLATES

BUFF TINGS

Buffalo chicken wings are a thing of sheer joy. That is, until your fingers are covered in hot sauce and blue cheese, and no amount of napkins can help you. These buffalo chicken bites are a much easier way to get your fix. Although there are a few steps to this recipe, they are easy to make at home. If you can't take the spice, the blue cheese sauce calms everything down.

Serves 4–6

800g (1¾lb) boneless chicken thigh or breast, diced into about 4cm (1½-inch) chunks
240ml (1 cup) buttermilk
500g (3¾ cups) gluten-free plain (all-purpose) flour
1 tbsp cayenne pepper
1 tbsp garlic powder
1 tbsp salt
Rapeseed (canola) or groundnut oil, for deep-frying

For the blue cheese sauce
100g (3½oz) Roquefort cheese, roughly chopped
300ml (1¼ cups) soured cream

For the hot sauce
85g (⅓ cup plus 2 tsp) unsalted butter
1 tsp cayenne pepper
1 tsp garlic powder
1 x 354ml (12oz) bottle of Frank's Original RedHot sauce

To serve
Chopped chives
Celery sticks

Place the diced chicken in a large bowl and pour over the buttermilk. Cover and refrigerate for at least 2 hours, or overnight if possible.

For the blue cheese sauce, put the Roquefort and soured cream in a pan and simmer over a low heat. Gently whisk together until combined; avoid bringing it to the boil. Remove and leave to cool.

For the hot sauce, melt the butter in a pan over a low heat. Add the cayenne, garlic powder and hot sauce. Heat through until it starts to simmer then take off the heat. Keep warm or reheat before serving.

Combine the flour, cayenne, garlic powder and salt in a deep tray and mix thoroughly. Remove the chicken from the buttermilk and coat in the seasoned flour before placing in a separate tray. Do this in small batches to avoid the flour getting too wet.

Heat the oil in a deep-fat fryer (or a deep, heavy saucepan, no more than two-thirds full) to 180°C/350°F. Add the chicken, in batches of about 6–8 pieces at a time, and fry for 4–6 minutes, until golden. A temperature probe should read 75°C/167°F. Toss the fried chicken in the warm hot sauce and serve with a sprinkling of chopped chives, alongside the celery sticks and blue cheese sauce for dipping.

AUBERGINE FRIES

WITH FETA & CHIPOTLE DIP

Deep-fried aubergine (eggplant) is great in many ways.
We love aubergine full stop and these fries are delicious and crispy.
The spicy, creamy and fresh dip complements them perfectly.
These are a firm favourite with our friends and family.

Serves 4

**For the aubergine
(eggplant) fries**
2 medium, firm aubergines
   (eggplants)
200g (1 ½ cups) gluten-free
   plain (all-purpose) flour
2 tsp salt
1 tsp cayenne pepper
100ml (7 tbsp) ice-cold
   sparkling water
Rapeseed (canola) or
   groundnut oil, for
   deep-frying

**For the feta &
chipotle dip**
200g (7oz) feta
2 tbsp finely chopped
   fresh mint
200ml (scant 1 cup)
   soured cream
2 tbsp chipotle
   en adobo paste

For the dip, crumble the feta in a bowl, add the
chopped mint, soured cream and chipotle en adobo
paste. Mix well to combine. (This keeps in an airtight
container in the refrigerator for up to 3 days, so can be
made in advance.)

Slice the aubergines (eggplants) into strips about 1cm
(⅜ inch) wide and 10cm (4 inches) long, leaving the
skin on. In a bowl, mix the flour, salt and cayenne. Add
the sparkling water a little at a time, whisking until it
forms a smooth batter.

Heat the oil in a deep-fat fryer (or a deep, heavy
saucepan, no more than two-thirds full) to 190°C/375°F.
Dip the aubergine strips in the batter and add, one at a
time, straight in to the hot oil. Do this in batches so you
don't overcrowd them. Cook for 2 minutes, until crispy
and golden. Remove to a plate lined with a paper towel.

Serve immediately with the feta & chipotle dip.

GMC SLAW

We love this fresh and zingy coleslaw as a side to our sandwiches. A perfect crunchy addition that also works well with the Buff tings on page 106.

Serves 8 as a side

2 medium carrots, grated
½ red cabbage, shredded
½ white cabbage, shredded
2 tbsp freshly chopped dill
6 tbsp mayonnaise
Juice of ½ lemon

Put the carrots, cabbage and dill in a large bowl. In a small bowl, combine the mayonnaise and lemon.

Stir the lemon mayo through the vegetables and serve immediately.

WATERMELON, FETA & CHILLI SALAD

This salad is best enjoyed fresh. It's quick and easy to make, perfect for a hot summer's day when you really can't be bothered to cook.

Serves 4

600g (1lb 5oz) watermelon
1 red chilli, finely diced
1 tbsp freshly chopped
  mint leaves
100g (3½oz) feta
Finely grated zest and
  juice of 1 lime
2 tbsp extra virgin olive oil

Cut the watermelon into slices 2cm (¾ inch) thick, and remove the skin from each slice. Chop the pink flesh into roughly 2cm (¾ inch) chunks and place in a serving bowl. Sprinkle the chilli and mint over the watermelon. Crumble the feta on top, followed by the lime zest and juice. Drizzle the extra virgin olive oil over and enjoy!

BABY GEM SALAD

This is a great salad. It's light and fresh with a
semi-creamy dressing, so it still feels a bit indulgent.

Serves 2

2 Baby Gem lettuces

For the dressing
175ml (¾ cup minus 1 tsp)
   buttermilk
1 tbsp mayonnaise
1 tbsp freshly chopped
   parsley
1 tbsp capers, chopped
1 garlic clove, crushed
½ tsp salt
½ tsp freshly ground pepper
Squeeze of lemon juice

Cut the bases off the Baby Gems and separate out
the leaves. Rinse in cold water and pat dry using
paper towels. Place in a serving dish.

To make the dressing, whisk all the ingredients
together in a bowl. Pour the dressing over the salad
and serve immediately.

CREAMY
TOMATO SOUP

Is there a more perfect pairing than comforting tomato
soup and gooey grilled cheese?

Serves 2–4

5 ripe tomatoes, quartered
1 tsp salt
1 tsp freshly ground pepper
2 tbsp olive oil
1 large onion, finely diced
2 garlic cloves, crushed
500ml (generous 2 cups)
  good vegetable or chicken
  stock
100ml (7 tbsp) double
  (heavy) cream

Preheat the oven to 190°C/375°F/Gas 5. Place
the tomatoes on a baking tray. Sprinkle over the salt,
pepper and 1 tablespoon of the oil. Roast in the
oven for 35–40 minutes, until puffed up and slightly
caramelized on the edges.

Heat the remaining oil in a large saucepan over
a gentle heat. Add the onion and cook slowly for
10 minutes, stirring, until soft and golden. Add the
garlic and cook for a further 2 minutes, before adding
the roasted tomatoes and stock. Let everything simmer
for 10 minutes.

Remove from the heat and leave to cool before
transferring to a blender. Blitz until smooth. Strain the
soup back into the pan, pushing as much of the pulp
through the sieve. Bring back to a gentle heat before
stirring in the cream.

Serve immediately, with a grilled cheese sandwich of
your choice.

CHEESE DUST

A sheer revelation. Use it in a GMC, sprinkled on top of
macaroni cheese or tossed with fries. The uses are endless! We
also use it in our Red pepper pesto on page 135.

**Makes about 300g
(3 cups)**

250g (8¾oz) Parmesan,
  finely grated (you can
  substitute a hard vegetarian
  cheese)
1 tbsp smoked paprika
1 tbsp garlic powder
1 tbsp freshly ground pepper
1 tbsp salt

Mix all the ingredients together and leave to sit for at
least an hour before using. Store in an airtight container
in the refrigerator for up to 2 weeks.

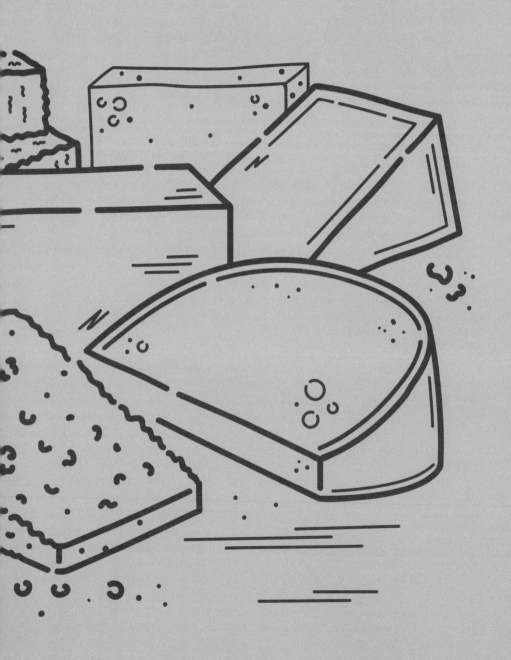

BEER CHEESE

This dip makes for a great starter or snack.
It's beery, spicy and smoky all at the same time.

**Makes about 1 litre
(4¼ cups)**

240ml (1 cup) beer,
preferably an IPA (we
use Big Hug Brewing's
Hibernation White), at room
temperature
200g (2 cups) grated mature
(sharp) Cheddar
200g (2 cups) grated red
Leicester cheese
1 tsp mustard powder
1 tsp smoked paprika
1 garlic clove, very finely
chopped
Salt (optional)

To serve
Freshly chopped parsley
Baguette, sliced and toasted

Pour the beer into a large bowl, whisk for 30 seconds
then leave to rest for 30 minutes. This is so that some
of the carbonation can be released.

Put the cheeses, spices and garlic into a food processor
with half of the beer. Process on a medium speed,
slowly adding the remaining beer as it starts to
combine. Scrape down the sides as you go to ensure
a smooth dip. Give it a taste and add salt if required
(this will depend on how salty the Cheddar is that you
have used).

Transfer to a bowl and serve with a sprinkling of
chopped parsley and toasted slices of baguette.

MOZZARELLA STICKS

What's not to love about mozzarella sticks? Crunchy, and melty with a serious cheese pull. These taste much better than any you will have ever eaten before. Make them fresh to impress.

Serves 4 as a snack or 2 as a starter

500g (1lb 2oz) mozzarella in a block
100g (2⅓ cups) panko breadcrumbs
1 tsp garlic powder
1 tsp salt
1 tsp Italian seasoning
1 egg
50g (6 tbsp) plain (all-purpose) flour
Rapeseed (canola) or groundnut (peanut) oil, for deep-frying

To serve
Slow-roasted tomato ketchup (see page 131)

Cut the mozzarella block into sticks about 1cm (⅜ inch) wide and 10cm (4 inches) long. Lay them out in a tray lined with baking parchment.

Put the breadcrumbs in a bowl. Give them a good crunch up with your hands so there is a mixture of finer and chunkier crumbs. Add the garlic powder, salt and Italian seasoning and mix to combine.

Crack the egg into a separate bowl and give it a light whisk. Put the flour into a third bowl. Line up the three bowls in order, so that you can have an easy assembly line. Dip each mozzarella stick in the flour, egg, then breadcrumbs, before placing back on your lined tray. Then dip each stick back in the egg and the breadcrumbs, to give them a double coating. This is really important: if they aren't properly coated in the breadcrumbs, the cheese will start to ooze out into the oil.

Heat the oil in a deep-fat fryer (or a deep, heavy saucepan, no more than two-thirds full), to 190°C/375°F. Add the coated mozzarella sticks to the hot oil, in batches. Cook for 2 minutes, until crispy and golden. Remove to a plate lined with paper towels. Serve immediately with our slow-roasted tomato ketchup.

POTATO SALAD

A quick and easy warm salad. This makes a great side
to any of our savoury sandwiches or at a barbecue.

Serves 4

750g (1½lb) new potatoes,
  scrubbed
120g (4¼oz) dry cure
  streaky (lean) bacon or
  pancetta, diced
½ red onion, finely sliced
1 tbsp finely snipped chives,
  to garnish

For the dressing
240ml (1 cup) buttermilk
2 tbsp mayonnaise
1 garlic clove, crushed
1 tsp smoked paprika
½ tsp salt
1 tsp freshly ground pepper
Squeeze of lemon juice

Cook the potatoes in boiling, salted water until tender.

Meanwhile, cook the bacon or pancetta in a frying
pan over a medium heat until nice and crisp. Remove
and set aside. Whisk together all the ingredients for
the dressing.

When the potatoes are cooked, drain, cut into quarters
and place in a serving dish. Sprinkle the crispy bacon
or pancetta on top followed by the sliced onion before
pouring over the dressing and tossing gently to coat.
Garnish with the chives and serve.

Salt 'n' Pepa's here! Have no fear.
Our sauces 'n' dips are better so drizzle
and sprinkle it real good.

CHEASONINGS

BBQ SAUCE

The best BBQ sauce you will ever taste. We know it's a bold claim, but even those who don't like BBQ sauce love this one. It's more sweet than smoky and is an absolute necessity in the Baby Got Mac (see page 50).

Makes 650ml (about 2¾ cups)

400ml (1⅔ cups) tomato ketchup
320ml (1⅓ cups) cola
110ml (½ cup minus 2 tsp) cider vinegar
80g (6½ tbsp) dark brown sugar
40ml (2 tbsp plus 2 tsp) treacle (blackstrap molasses)
1½ tbsp onion powder
1½ tbsp garlic powder
1½ tbsp freshly ground pepper
1½ tsp ground allspice

Combine all the ingredients in a saucepan and place over a medium heat. Stir constantly for 5 minutes, until everything comes together. Reduce the heat to low and simmer for 20–30 minutes, stirring occasionally. The sauce should be thick and coat the back of a spoon when ready. Allow to cool then store in sterilized bottles in the refrigerator. It will keep for up to 8 weeks.

BÉCHAMEL

We put a béchamel in our classic grilled cheese, the GMC (see page 22). It adds an extra richness and creaminess to your classic toastie. It will store in the refrigerator for up to 4 days.

Makes 600ml (2½ cups)

50g (3½ tbsp) unsalted butter
50g (6 tbsp) plain (all-purpose) flour
570ml (scant 2½ cups) whole milk
100g (3½oz) mature (sharp) Cheddar, grated

Melt the butter in a pan over a low heat before whisking in the flour. Let the flour cook out for a couple of minutes, stirring continuously.

In a separate pan, heat the milk over a medium heat without bringing it to the boil. Slowly add the warmed milk to the butter and flour roux. Whisk continuously to avoid any lumps. Let the sauce thicken over a low- medium heat, before adding the cheese and stirring until fully incorporated.

SLOW-ROASTED
TOMATO KETCHUP

Slow roasting tomatoes really intensifies their flavour.
This comes through in the ketchup. It's rich, sweet and tangy.
Dip your chips in it (or your cheese toasties).

Makes 500ml
(generous 2 cups)

1.5kg (3lb 5oz) vine tomatoes
(about 10–12 tomatoes)
1 large onion, peeled and cut
into wedges
4 large garlic cloves, peeled
3 tbsp olive oil
1 tsp salt
½ tsp freshly ground pepper
2 tbsp black treacle
(blackstrap molasses)
3 tbsp tomato paste
100g (½ cup) brown sugar
120ml (½ cup) red wine
vinegar

Preheat oven to 180°C/350°F/Gas 4. Cut the tomatoes in half and place in a deep baking tray. Add the onion, whole garlic cloves, oil and salt and pepper. Toss everything together to coat. Keep the tomatoes in a single layer, cut side up. Roast for 40 minutes, until the tomatoes are puffed up.

Remove and leave to cool. Tip into a blender (make sure you get all the juice from the tray). Add the treacle (molasses), tomato paste, sugar and vinegar. Blend until smooth.

Place a sieve over a large pan and strain the tomato mixture through it. Use a spoon to push as much of the mixture through the sieve as you can.

Place over a low heat and simmer for 1 hour. Stir occasionally until it has reduced to a thick, deep red sauce. It will splatter quite a bit, so if you have a mesh screen, put this on top.

Leave to cool before transferring into sterilized jars or an airtight container. It will keep in the refrigerator for up to 3 weeks.

SCOTCH BONNET &
RED PEPPER JAM

Use this jam (jelly) in the PB&J on page 74. It works really well on a cheese board, or even tossed through a noodle salad for a sweet and spicy kick.

Makes 1.5 litres (6½ cups)

150g (5¼oz) red chillies, deseeded and roughly chopped
2 red Scotch bonnet chillies, roughly chopped
150g (5¼oz) red (bell) peppers, deseeded and roughly chopped
1kg (5 cups) jam (jelly) sugar
600ml (2½ cups) cider vinegar

Put the chopped chillies and red (bell) peppers into a food processer and pulse until finely chopped.

In a medium pan, dissolve the sugar in the vinegar over a low heat, without stirring.

Scrape the chilli and pepper mixture into the pan and bring to the boil. Leave at a rolling boil, without stirring, for 10 minutes. Remove from the heat and allow to cool. Be very careful not to touch the mixture, as it will be extremely hot.

As it cools, the liquid will become more jam (jelly) like. After 40 minutes, the flecks of chilli and pepper will be evenly dispersed. At this point, ladle it into sterilized jars. It will keep in the refrigerator for 2 months.

CANDY BACON
BUTTER

There is nothing like bacon for breakfast (or any time of the day for that matter). We make this candy bacon butter to go into the Kim Candashian on page 52. You can store it in the fridge and get your bacon fix at any time of the day without even taking out your frying pan! Our take on this bacon jam is deep in flavour, and a little goes a long way.

Makes 700g (1lb 9oz)

600g (1lb 5oz) unsmoked streaky (lean) bacon, cut into thick strips about 12mm (½-inch) wide
2 large white onions, sliced
125g (⅔ cup minus 2 tsp) dark brown sugar
100ml (7 tbsp) freshly brewed espresso (instant works too)
100ml (7 tbsp) water
1 tbsp balsamic vinegar

Put the bacon in a large saucepan over a medium-high heat and cook. Stir, until cooked but still quite chewy (not crispy). Remove the bacon to a plate, leaving the rendered fat in the pan.

Add the onions to the bacon fat and cook over a medium heat for 10 minutes. Reduce the heat to low and cook until tender. Stir in the sugar and continue to cook until the onions have caramelized. Add the espresso and water to the pan, with the cooked bacon. Cook until everything comes together and is jammy. This will take 15 minutes. Remove from the heat and stir through the vinegar.

Leave to cool then blitz to your desired smoothness in a food processor; we like to leave ours a bit chunky. Store in sterilized jars, in the refrigerator (where it will keep for 2 weeks), or in an airtight container if you plan to eat it all within a week.

LEMON, BASIL &

WALNUT PESTO

This is our take on a very classic pesto Genovese, but instead of creamy pine nuts, we use walnuts. This changes the texture. We use this in the Hey Pesto sandwich on page 28, but it's great with pasta, salads and roasted vegetables.

Makes about 600ml (2½ cups)

50g (⅓ cup) walnut halves
2 garlic cloves, roughly chopped
Grated zest and juice of 1 lemon
100g (3½oz) fresh basil leaves
300ml (1¼ cups) extra virgin olive oil
½ tsp salt
½ tsp freshly ground pepper
75g (2¾oz) Parmesan, freshly grated

Preheat the oven to 200°C/400°F/Gas 6. Spread the walnuts on a baking tray. Toast in the oven for 10 minutes, shaking the tray halfway through.

Put the garlic, toasted walnuts and lemon zest in a food processor and blitz together. Add the lemon juice, basil leaves and half the oil and blitz again. Add the rest of the oil and the salt and pepper and blitz once more. Scrape into a bowl and stir the grated Parmesan through. Store in a jar in the refrigerator for up to a week.

PESTO

This is essentially a meat-free version of 'nduja (a soft, spicy spreadable salami from Italy). It is sweet, spicy and smoky. It works really well with pretty much everything! You can use it in pasta, as a base for flatbreads or in one of our favourite toasties (see page 34).

Makes about 660ml (2¾ cups)

3 red (bell) peppers
150ml (10 tbsp) extra virgin olive oil, plus a drizzle for the peppers
85g (⅔ cup) hazelnuts
100g (¾ cup) cheese dust (see page 117)
30g (1oz) Parmesan or vegetarian hard cheese, freshly grated
Cayenne pepper, to taste
Good pinch of salt

Preheat the oven to 200°C/400°F/Gas 6. Rinse the (bell) peppers, and pat dry. Place in a roasting dish and rub with oil. Roast for 30 minutes, until the skins have blackened and blistered. Remove from the oven and transfer the peppers to a plastic food bag. Seal and leave for 10 minutes to allow them to sweat and make the skins easily removable.

Meanwhile, toast the hazelnuts on a baking tray in the oven for 8–10 minutes, keeping an eye on them so they don't burn. Remove and leave to cool before blitzing in a small food processor or spice grinder, until fine-medium ground.

Once the peppers have cooled, remove from the plastic bag along with the juices (keep these). Peel off the skins and discard, along with the stalks and any core.

Put the juices and peppers into a food processor and blitz to a smooth purée. Scrape the purée into a mixing bowl and stir in the ground hazelnuts, Cheese dust, grated cheese, cayenne pepper, salt and remaining oil. Mix well and either use straight away or store in a sterilized jar for up to 2 weeks.

CORIANDER, APPLE &

PEANUT CHUTNEY

This is a great fresh chutney that we put in to the Slumdog Grillionaire on page 78. It also makes for a great dip, served with crudités.

Makes 500g (4 cups)

50g (⅓ cup) red-skinned peanuts
15g (½oz) fresh root ginger, roughly chopped
1 garlic clove, roughly chopped
2 green finger chillies, roughly chopped
1 tsp cumin seeds
150ml (10 tbsp) water
1 Granny Smith apple, cored and chopped
½ tsp salt
1 tbsp caster (superfine) sugar
100g (3½oz) coriander (cilantro) leaves
Grated zest of 1 lime and juice of 1½

Preheat oven to 180°C/350°F/Gas 4. Spread the peanuts out on a baking tray and roast for 10 minutes, shaking the tray halfway through. The skins should fall off easily. Set aside to cool.

Put the peanuts into a food processor and pulse until as fine as possible. Remove and set aside.

Add the ginger, garlic, chillies and cumin seeds to the processor and pulse until everything is finely chopped. Add 3 tablespoons of the water and pulse again. Add the chopped apple, salt and sugar, and pulse. Add the coriander (cilantro) and the lime zest and juice and pulse again until mostly chopped. Add the remaining 7 tablespoons of water and pulse until almost smooth, then add the ground peanuts and pulse for the last time.

This is a fresh chutney, so should be eaten on the day. It will keep for up to 3 days in the refrigerator.

RED ONION
CONFIT

The sweet, rich onion confit works well with goat's cheese, terrines and on a cheese board. It's an essential ingredient in our Confit West toastie on page 55.

Makes 500g (1½ cups)

50g (3½ tbsp) unsalted butter
1 tbsp extra virgin olive oil
3 medium red onions, sliced
120ml (½ cup) red wine
75g (6 tbsp) brown sugar
50ml (3½ tbsp) balsamic
   vinegar
½ tsp salt
½ tsp freshly ground pepper

Melt the butter and oil together in a saucepan over a low-medium heat. Add the onions and cook until softened but not browned, about 8–10 minutes.

Add the wine and sugar and cook for another 30 minutes over a low heat, stirring occasionally to avoid any burning. If the mixture is drying out too quickly, you can add a touch more wine. Once the onions are tender, add the vinegar and cook for another 5 minutes, letting it all absorb into the onions. The onions should look silky and deep purple in colour. Stir in the salt and pepper.

Store in an airtight container for up to 5 days in the refrigerator.

INDEX

"Some people are worth melting for" Olaf, *Frozen* 2013

To our mums and grandmothers, thank you for your love, recipes and patience.
To our bodies, thank you for not making us lactose intolerant.
To our fellow cheese lovers, we thank you all.
In a world full of uncertainty, we will always have cheese.

Publishing Director: Sarah Lavelle
Creative Director: Helen Lewis
Project Editor: Amy Christian
Copy Editor: Sally Somers
Design Concept: Agostino Carrea
Designer: Emily Lapworth
Photography: Martin Poole
Food Stylist: Kim Morphew
Prop Stylist: Rachel Jukes
Production: Tom Moore, Vincent Smith

First published in 2017 by Quadrille Publishing
Pentagon House, 52–54 Southwark Street,
London SE1 1UN

Quadrille Publishing is an
imprint of Hardie Grant
www.hardiegrant.com.au
www.quadrille.co.uk

Text © 2017 Nisha Patel & Nishma Chauhan
Photography © 2017 Martin Poole
Photography on page 7 © 2017 Ioana Marinca
Design and layout © 2017 Quadrille Publishing

Cataloguing in Publication Data:
a catalogue record for this book is
available from the British Library.

ISBN: 978 184949 942 2

Printed in China